HOW TO BUILD A
PLANE

© 2015 Quarto Publishing Group USA Inc.
Published by Walter Foster Jr., an imprint of Quarto Publishing Group USA Inc.
All rights reserved. Walter Foster Jr. is trademarked.
Artwork © Martin Sodomka
Written by Saskia Lacey
Illustrated by Martin Sodomka

Publisher: Anne Landa
Creative Director: Shelley Baugh
Production Director: Yuhong Guo
Editorial Director: Pauline Molinari
Senior Editor: Stephanie Meissner
Managing Editor: Karen Julian
Associate Editor: Jennifer Gaudet
Project Editor: Heidi Fiedler
Editorial Assistant: Julie Chapa
Production Designer: Debbie Aiken

Special thanks to Cory Graff for his high-flying expertise

www.walterfoster.com
6 Orchard Road, Suite 100
Lake Forest, CA 92630

Printed in China, June 2015
1 3 5 7 9 10 8 6 4 2
1768

HOW TO BUILD A
PLANE

Written by SASKIA LACEY

Illustrated by MARTIN SODOMKA

TABLE OF CONTENTS

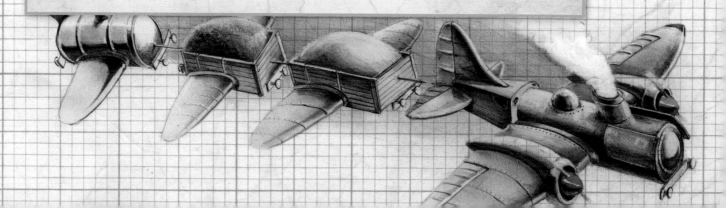

MEET THE SCRAP PACK!

Eli

The Dreamer

A mouse with an elephant-sized imagination.

Most likely to: Have his head in the clouds

Flying style: Adventurous

Phoebe
The Expert
The inside source on flying (having wings helps)!
Most likely to: Know what's what
Flying style: Natural

Hank
The Supply Guy
The frog with a fantastic fear of heights.
Most likely to: Find a junkyard gem
Flying style: Prefers life on the ground

Step 1: Imagine

Eli knew he was a mouse. Tail? Check. Whiskers? Check. Big ears? Double check. But secretly, Eli wondered if he might be part bird. What else could explain his total obsession with flying? He dreamed of sailing on the wind and getting a close-up of the clouds. Eli had what animals call a serious case of "wing envy." And it didn't help that his best friend was a bird.

Eli knew the closest he could get to flying was in a plane. But he didn't just want to fly in one, he wanted to build one. It was a huge project, but Eli was known for his big imagination—and his crazy ideas. When his friends Phoebe and Hank pitched in, sometimes his projects even worked! The only problem was convincing them to help.

"Phoebe, how do you feel about building a plane?" Eli asked hopefully.

"A plane?" Phoebe gave her friend a strange look. "Why would I build a plane? I have wings." Phoebe laughed and flapped her wings playfully at the mouse.

9

Phoebe had a point. Building a plane didn't make much sense for a bird. But maybe Hank would help.

"A plane?" Hank scrunched up his face. "I don't know. I really don't like heights." Hank was scared of everything. "My legs are made for jumping from rock to rock, not cloud to cloud."

"Come on," Eli pleaded. "Flying is like taking one big jump. The world's biggest jump."

But Hank just shook his head nervously. Eli could tell the frog wasn't going anywhere in a plane anytime soon.

Eli had nearly given up when he got a lucky break. Phoebe changed her mind! Her curiosity had finally gotten the best of her, and she came to talk to Eli.

"I've been wondering…do you think a plane's wings work like my wings?" she asked.

"There's one way to find out," said Eli.

Phoebe raised her beak in the air thoughtfully. "We did make a pretty good team when we built that car. Maybe we can do it again."

Eli squeaked. "I'm so glad you're going to help! This is going to be amazing!"

"I didn't say yes yet!" Phoebe objected.

"Phoebes, you're in. I can tell you're in!" Eli was jumping up and down.

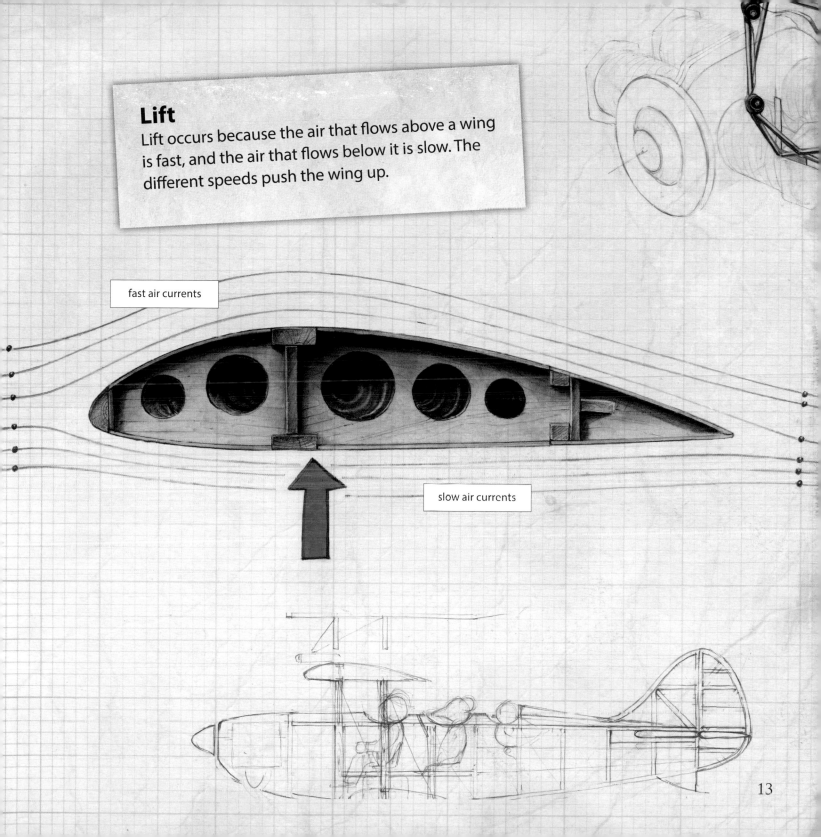

Lift

Lift occurs because the air that flows above a wing is fast, and the air that flows below it is slow. The different speeds push the wing up.

fast air currents

slow air currents

13

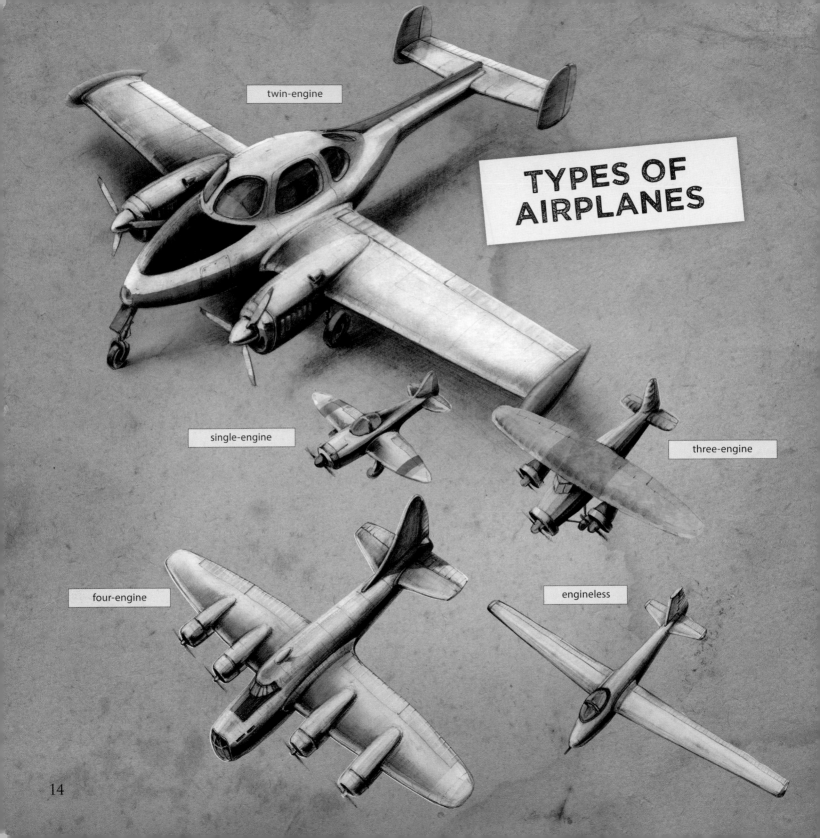

twin-engine

TYPES OF
AIRPLANES

single-engine

three-engine

four-engine

engineless

14

low wing

mid wing

high wing

biplane

single-seater,
twenty-three-engine
multiplane

With Phoebe on board, Eli could really start dreaming. What kind of plane would they build? A monoplane with one wing would be easy, but a biplane with two wings would have greater lift. The stronger the lift, the more weight the plane could carry. If they built a biplane, Eli could take friends along on his flying adventures.

Eli obsessed over the engines. He was pretty sure more was more when it came to engines. Should there be two or three? Or maybe twenty-three?!

Step 2: Build a Model

The next day, Eli pitched his monster plane to Phoebe.

"Twenty-three engines?" Phoebe sputtered. "There's NO way. Let's start small. In fact, maybe our first plane shouldn't have an engine at all."

"No engine? How will we get it off the ground?" Eli asked.

"We can build a glider. It will only be able to carry one flier, but it will help us learn more about how a plane works. If we can get a glider in the air, then we can talk about engines."

Eli and Phoebe set to work on the model. As they were finishing up the wings, Hank showed up.

"Buddy!" Eli cried. "Are you joining the team?"

"I still don't want to fly," Hank said. "But I will help you guys build. I came across an engine in the junkyard that I think might be perfect for a plane."

An engine! Eli grinned at Phoebe.

She rolled her eyes and said, "Alright boys, let's get this glider up in the air!"

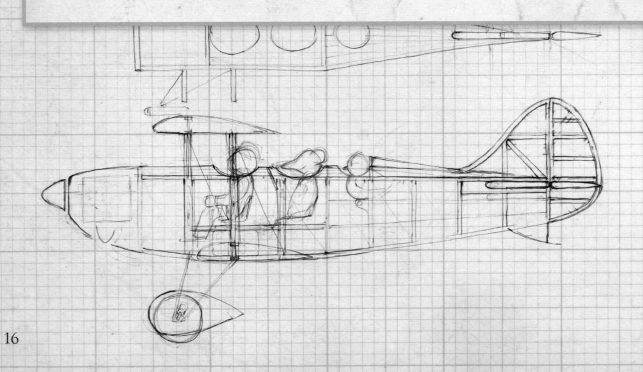

Making a Plan

Engineers sketch how a plane will look before they ever start building. Taking time to draw all the parts and pieces lets them think through the project and problem-solve while they're safely on the ground.

17

FLYING PRACTICE

Hank and Phoebe fussed over Eli as they hooked him into the glider.

"Are you sure you're ready for this?" Hank asked.

"I've been dreaming about it forever." Eli replied. "Strap me in!"

Secure in the seat, Eli began to run, pulling the glider behind him. Then, with a push from Hank, the wings were in the air.

Eli couldn't believe it. He wasn't far off the ground, and he had to be careful— the glider was flimsy —but he was flying!

"You guys, it's working!" Eli cried.

Hank skipped alongside the plane, while Phoebe hooted with glee.

With new enthusiasm, the friends began to build again. The glider had worked. Now they could build a real plane with an engine. But before they could build the engine, they would need to assemble the fuselage.

Eli and Hank weren't sure what a fuselage was or how to build it. Luckily, Phoebe had done her homework. She explained the fuselage was like a skeleton that held the plane together. The cockpit was at the front, and the passengers were in the back. The three friends began to assemble the wood frame.

ASSEMBLING THE FRAME

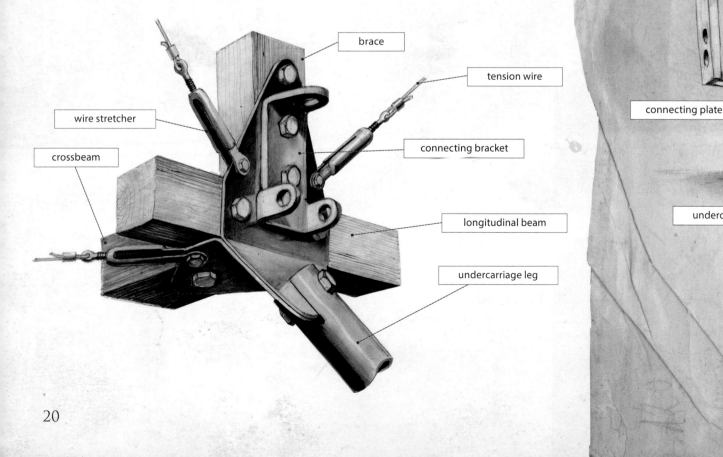

brace

tension wire

wire stretcher

connecting bracket

crossbeam

longitudinal beam

undercarriage leg

connecting plate

undercarriage leg

FUSELAGE

The next day, Eli brought a few friends to help them build the plane. He wanted to take off as soon as possible.

"Hank, how are we looking on the engine?" Eli asked.

"I've found some good stuff." Hank paused. "I've also found a lot of junk."

Eli groaned. "I thought you said you had found the perfect engine?"

"Don't worry, Eli. I won't let you down," Hank smiled and gave a little hop.

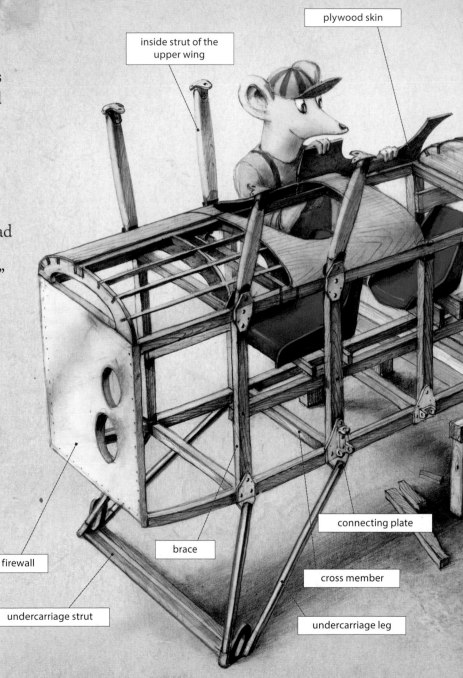

plywood skin

inside strut of the upper wing

connecting plate

brace

cross member

firewall

undercarriage strut

undercarriage leg

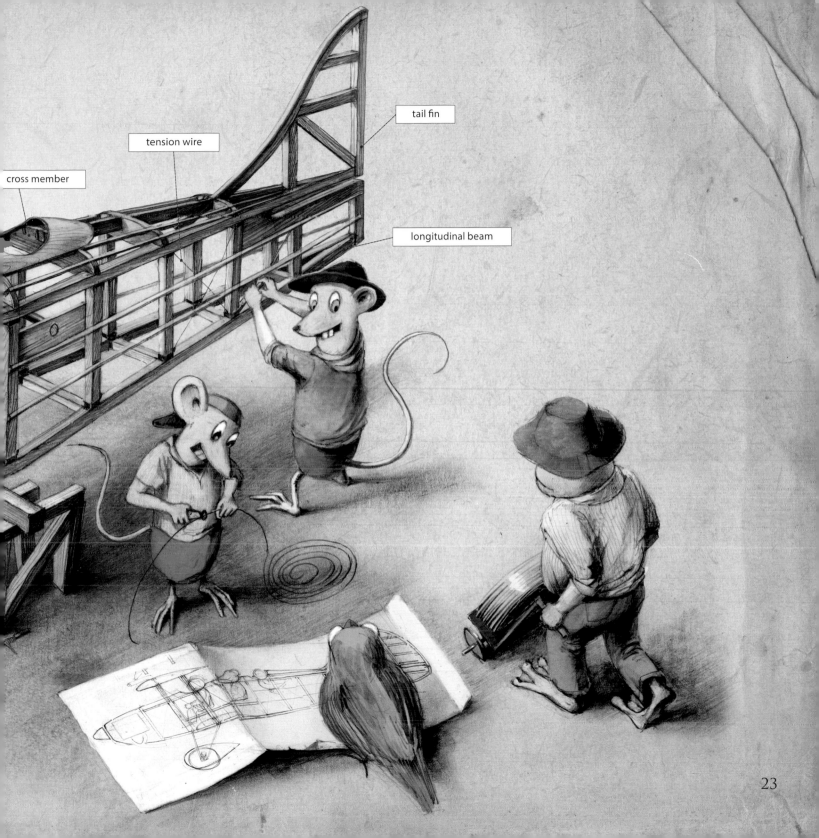

cross member

tension wire

tail fin

longitudinal beam

23

Step 3: Build the Wings

Soon Phoebe was giving the Scrap Pack a wing tutorial. "We need to cover the leading edge of the wing with plywood, as far as the spar. That will strengthen the wing. Then we'll sand down everything, so there aren't any bumps when we cover the whole plane with fabric."

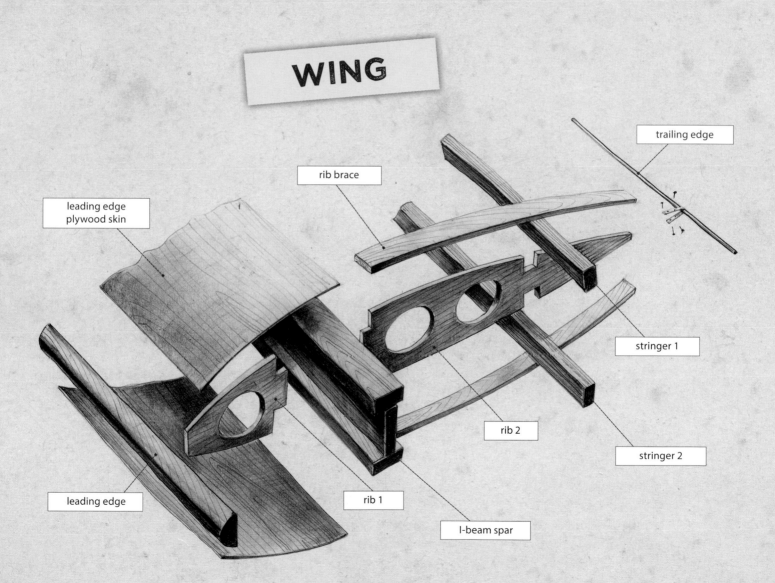

WING

leading edge plywood skin

rib brace

trailing edge

stringer 1

stringer 2

rib 2

leading edge

rib 1

I-beam spar

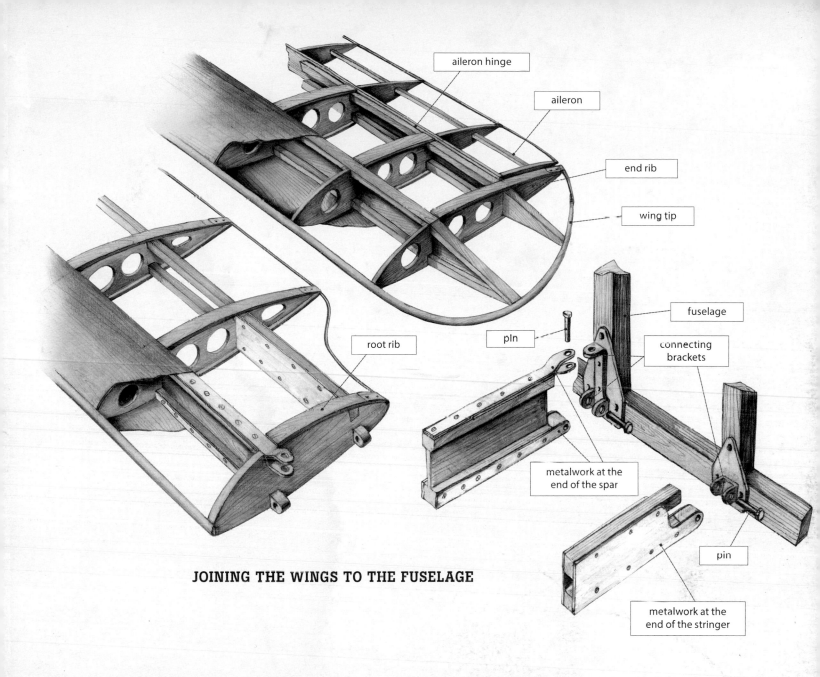

aileron hinge

aileron

end rib

wing tip

fuselage

pIn

connecting
brackets

root rib

metalwork at the
end of the spar

pin

metalwork at the
end of the stringer

JOINING THE WINGS TO THE FUSELAGE

"How are we going to attach the wings to the fuselage?" Hank asked.

"Well, it's pretty simple," Phoebe began. "The wing is attached to the fuselage with three brackets."

"Sounds secure to me," Hank admitted.

"Awesome, let's get started!" Eli said excitedly.

After a hard day's work, Eli went home and thought about all the things he would do once the plane was finished. Maybe he would become Eli Knievel, Stunt Pilot! Eli imagined himself somersaulting through the air, diving dangerously close to the ground, and then, at the last second, climbing back up, up, UP!

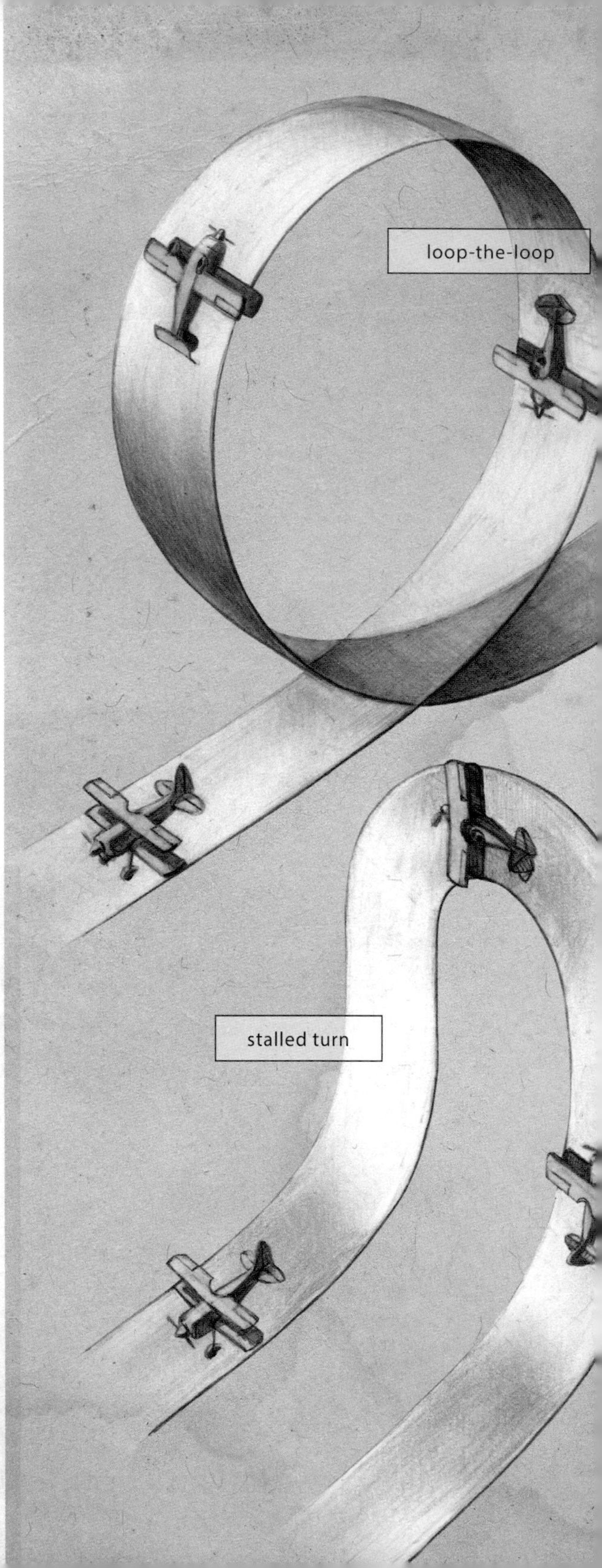

loop-the-loop

stalled turn

FLIPS AND TRICKS

roll

Immelmann turn

half-roll

The following day was dedicated to building the tail. Everyone was starting to get tired, but Eli did his best to encourage the crew.

"We can do this," he said. "We just need to finish the tail and the engine. Think of all the places we'll go. France! Thailand! Zimbabwe!"

"Do we really need a tail?" Hank grumbled. "I don't see the point."

"Yes, Hank." Phoebe flapped a wing tiredly.

Eli added, "The tail of a plane works just like Phoebe's tail. It's what makes the plane stable. You don't want us to crash do you?"

"Don't even say that!" Hank moaned.

hinge

vertical stabilizer

rudder

tail fin

stabilizer

horizontal stabilizer

elevator

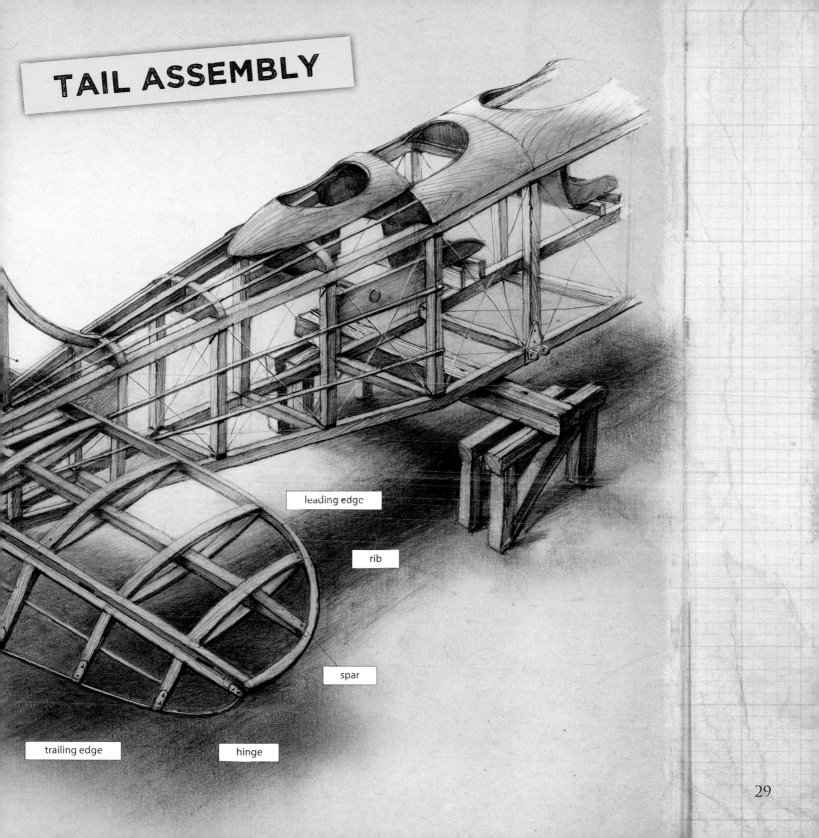

TAIL ASSEMBLY

leading edge

rib

spar

trailing edge

hinge

ENGINE

propeller shaft

toothed rim

starter gear

cylinder, cylinder head, and cooling fins

pushrod cover

high-voltage cable

spark plug

exhaust pipe

Step 4: Build the Engine

When it was time for the engine, Hank came through for the pack. The engine he found had four cylinders and a double ignition. That meant there were two spark plugs for every cylinder, so the engine would be very reliable. Hank had found them the safest engine in the junkyard.

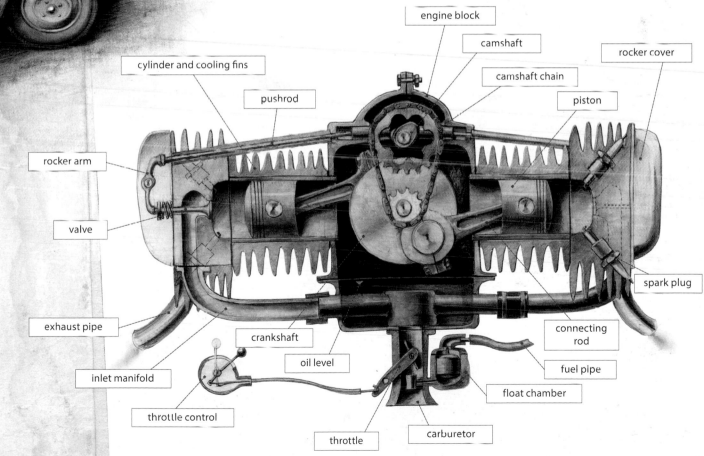

Now that they had the engine, they could mount it on the plane. Meanwhile, Phoebe was working on the propeller.

"I think it's amazingly well-balanced, if I do say so myself," Phoebe chirped triumphantly. "Believe me, that's a good thing. If the propeller isn't balanced, the whole plane will shake. "The propeller is what drives the plane into the air."

"Well done, Phoebes!" Eli squeaked.

The team worked together to connect the engine and propeller to the body of the plane.

ENGINE BOX

lattice structure

silent block bush

MOUNTING THE ENGINE

cylinder

engine compartment

propeller driveshaft

propeller

starter motor

exhaust pipe

carburetor

fuel tank

33

There was so much to learn about flying. Eli didn't know where to begin. He tried to read a book Phoebe had given him about handling a plane, but he was too excited about flying to pay much attention.

aileron

aileron

Banking

Handling a plane isn't as easy as driving a car. With a plane, even something that looks simple can be complicated. When a plane turns, it's called "banking." In order to do this successfully, the pilot must handle multiple controls at the same time. The *ailerons* cause the wings to tip to the left or right. They make the plane bank, or turn.

IN-AIR ACTION

Climbing
The elevator is like a pair of small wings. The pilot can control the elevator to help the plane dive downward or climb upward.

elevator

rudder

Turning
The rudder helps keep the turns controlled, so the plane doesn't zig or zag. In other words, the rudder helps the plane stay on course.

AERODYNAMICS

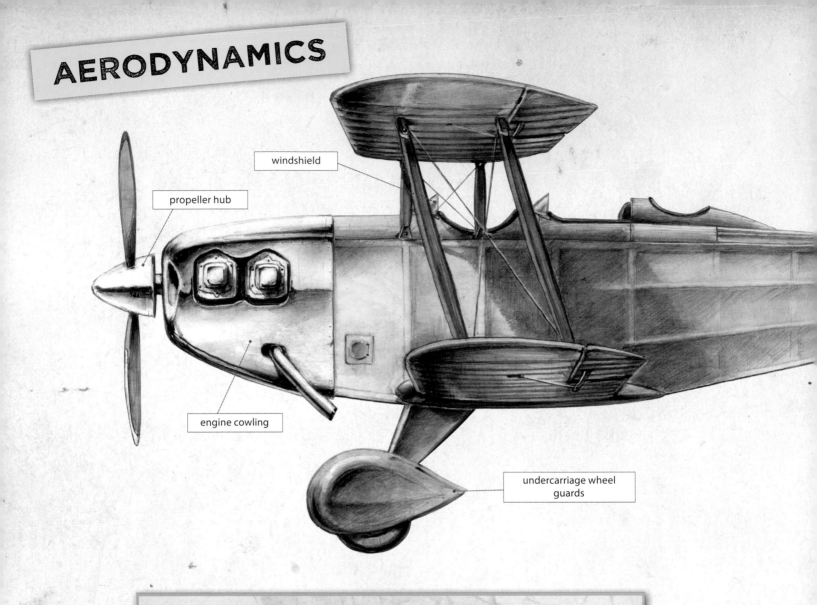

propeller hub

windshield

engine cowling

undercarriage wheel guards

As Eli studied the physics of flying, his mind began to wander. If he was going to be a stunt pilot, he should probably get a parachute. How cool would it be to skydive from his own plane?!?

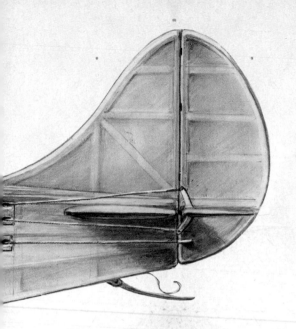

Aerodynamics

Air is what makes flying possible—it creates lift. But it also makes flying difficult. Think about how hard it is to run against a strong gust of wind, and planes have to move much faster against the wind than we run! Engineers work hard to make planes aerodynamic, shaping them so they move as smoothly as possible through the air.

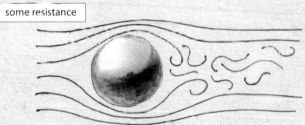

little resistance

some resistance

strong resistance

PARACHUTE

COVERING THE PLANE

Back in the garage, Eli and the rest of the crew were making good progress. They began covering the aircraft with linen.

"Are you excited for the test flight?" asked Phoebe.

"Excited, yes. And a little scared," Eli confessed. "But don't tell Hank. I still think we can get him in that plane, and I don't want him to get so scared that he hops out!"

Phoebe giggled. "I can't wait to see that frog fly!"

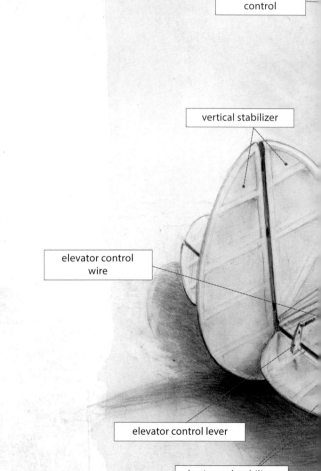

outside strut

upper aileron control

vertical stabilizer

elevator control wire

elevator control lever

horizontal stabilizer

upper wing

inside strut

propeller

engine

lower wing

aileron control wire

aileron control lever

rib

spar

pulley

stringer

aileron

canvas covering

39

Eli was in charge of designing the cockpit. After all, he was the one who would be piloting the plane! He looked carefully at each of the flight instruments. They would be his trusted advisors while he was flying. If something went wrong, they would let him know.

Fuel

Propeller planes require gasoline to fly. This isn't the same gas a car uses. Aviation fuel has a higher standard of purity and is more reliable.

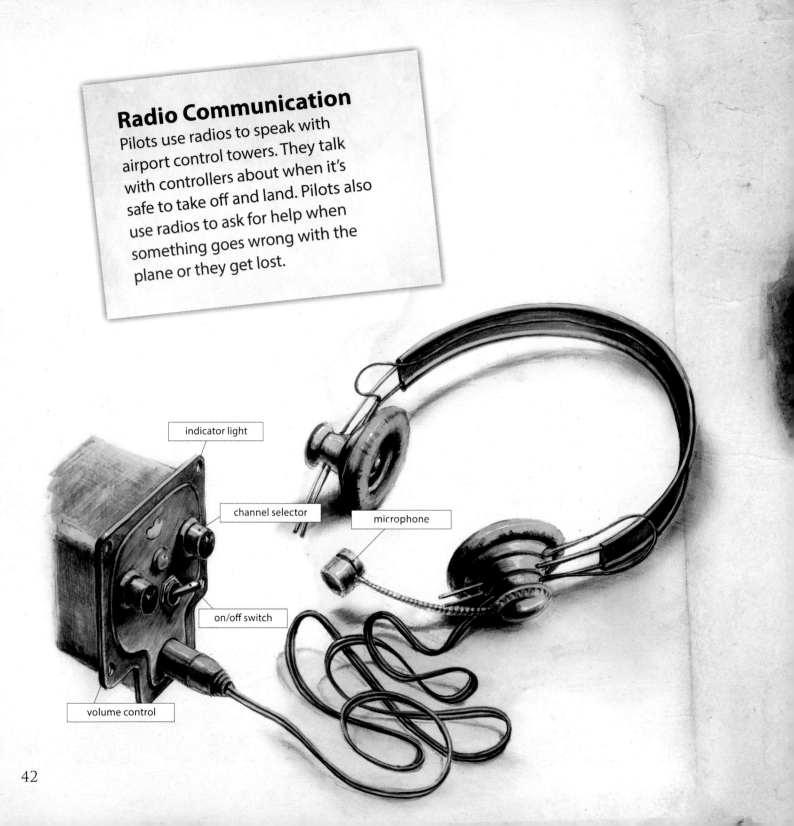

Radio Communication

Pilots use radios to speak with airport control towers. They talk with controllers about when it's safe to take off and land. Pilots also use radios to ask for help when something goes wrong with the plane or they get lost.

indicator light

channel selector

microphone

on/off switch

volume control

PAINTING THE PLANE

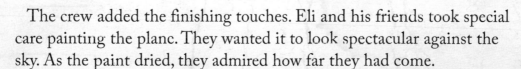

    The crew added the finishing touches. Eli and his friends took special care painting the plane. They wanted it to look spectacular against the sky. As the paint dried, they admired how far they had come.

After weeks of hard work, the plane was ready for its first test flight.

"Ready, copilot?" Eli grinned.

"Ready!" Phoebe said and hopped on board.

Hank checked the sky nervously, "I don't know if you should fly. I heard that there might be strong winds today."

"Oh, Hank," Eli shook his head. "We'll be fine!"

"Check your flight instruments—" Hank began.

"Don't worry! I've got a parachute and Phoebe has wings," said Eli.

Hank sighed, "Fine, but no sky-diving!"

Phoebe coached the mouse throughout takeoff. "We've got to fly against the wind. So turn the plane around slowly," Phoebe instructed. "Now go full-throttle!"

Eli's stomach twisted and turned. Could he really do this? The plane shook as it gained speed. Eli felt the plane lift into the air. It was happening. They were…

FLYING! Eli and Phoebe cheered as the plane climbed through the air. They flew higher and higher until Hank was just a spot of green on the ground.

This is so easy, thought Eli. *I knew I was part bird!* "Don't go too high," Phoebe warned. "Remember what Hank said. The wind is stronger up here."

But Eli didn't listen. He was too excited to hear Phoebe.

"Eli, take us down. You're losing control."

"Don't worry, Phoebes." The mouse cheered, "I'm at one with the wind!"

"No, it's too strong. We're going to—"

The plane took a sickening turn. A powerful wind threw the small plane upside down and sideways. Eli panicked, he couldn't tell which direction was up or down. They were going to crash!

"Mayday! Mayday!" Eli shouted into the radio.

"Eli! What's happening?" Hank called back.

"He's losing control of the plane," Phoebe shouted.

"Look at your flight instruments," said Hank. "What do you see?"

Eli read back everything he saw to Hank.

"You've got to level out!" the frog croaked. He began to read Eli instructions from a flight manual. Eli did his best to follow along, twisting and turning each of the instruments until they improved. As the levels changed, he stayed focused. Somehow he managed to guide the plane to a soft patch of grass. They landed with a thud that shook their bones, but they were safe!

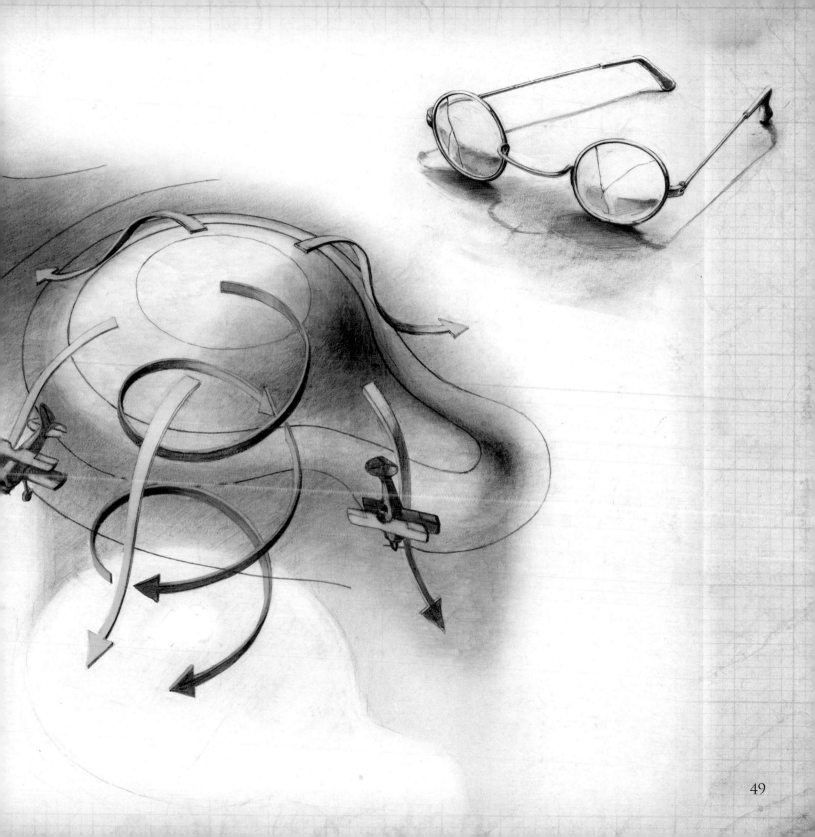

The two friends scrambled out of the plane, both relieved to be back on solid ground. Hank ran towards them. He looked even more scared than Eli or Phoebe. "That did NOT cure my fear of heights," the frog wheezed.

"I'm so sorry, Hank," said Eli. "I should have listened to you. Flying was an awful idea."

"That's not true," said Phoebe. "We just need to prepare better."

Eli shook his head sadly, "No, it's ok. I'm a mouse, I don't belong in the air."

Phoebe elbowed Hank. "Say something!"

Hank looked at the mouse. Eli tugged on a whisker sadly.

Hank sighed, "Maybe we could try again. I actually had some ideas about how you could angle your takeoff more like a jump so you don't have such a rocky start."

"Really?" Eli trembled with excitement. "You want to try again? I'll more careful this time. I promise no more stunts in the air!"

"Let's start studying." Phoebe smiled.

Hank gathered some manuals from his shop. Phoebe, Eli, and Hank each took turns reading.

"First off, it's a good idea to learn about weather patterns if we plan on flying long distances," Phoebe said. "We should check the wind speed before we leave the ground."

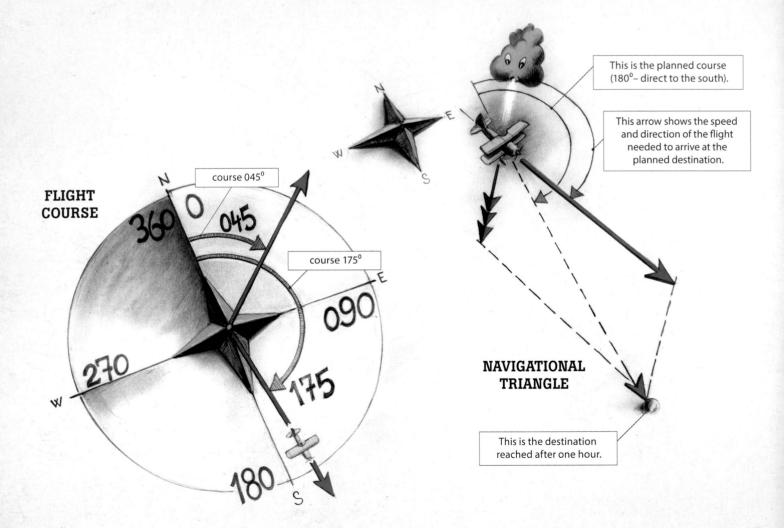

FLIGHT COURSE

course 045°

course 175°

NAVIGATIONAL TRIANGLE

This is the planned course (180°– direct to the south).

This arrow shows the speed and direction of the flight needed to arrive at the planned destination.

This is the destination reached after one hour.

final point of the route

NAVIGATION

170

120

220

turning point of the route

course

175

starting point of the route

course line

A windsock shows the wind's direction and strength.

Using a Map
Pilots use a map to plan their flight paths. They need to know where to refuel and where they can land safely.

After a crash course in weather, Phoebe and Eli felt ready to try again. Hank stared at the plane, but he still wasn't sure flying was for him.

"Don't just sit there and watch. Climb aboard, friend!" Eli called.

Hank wrung his hands nervously.

"We'll be fine!" Phoebe called to Hank. "You've seen all the work we've put in to this. We're ready."

"But what if we crash?" Hank asked.

"We won't crash if you're along! You're the one who got us out of that tailspin the last time," Eli assured him. He started the engine. "Just think—you'll be the world's first flying frog! You can travel to the greatest junkyards on earth."

"Well, there could be some unusual motorcycle parts out there. Things I've never seen before," said Hank. "I've always wanted to build a bike." Eli nodded vigorously. Hank straightened his tie. "You know, Eli, you don't just dream up these crazy schemes. You get me dreaming up crazy schemes too." Eli opened his mouth to apologize, but the frog cut him off. "I kind of like it," Hank admitted.

"Well, then, that's what friends are for," the mouse replied.

Phoebe chirped her agreement. Eli was the best friend they could ever hope for. "Jump in, Hank!" With that, he hopped in to the front seat.

55

Step 5: Take to the Sky!

The three friends prepared for takeoff. Eli checked the flight instruments carefully, keeping his eye on them as they climbed.

"Looking good!" Phoebe cheered.

"Thanks, Phoebes. I think I'm starting to get the hang of it."

Hank croaked happily, "Just don't try to talk me into skydiving."

As they leveled off, Eli let himself take a breath and look around. The view was spectacular. He had his best friends by his side. They could go anywhere they wanted. Make anything they dared. And dream ENORMOUS pie-in-the-sky-sized dreams!

The Scrap Pack spent the rest of the day in the sky. No one—not even Hank—wanted to come down.

FLIGHT INSTRUMENTS

compass

airspeed indicator

turn-and-bank indicator

Flying 101

If you want to fly like Eli, here are a few things you'll need to know before you climb into the cockpit.

Airspeed Indicator

Compares the plane's speed to the surrounding air. The red area shows high speeds that are dangerous to the plane's structure. If the pilot flies too fast, the plane may be damaged.

Compass

Tells the direction of the plane's present course. At least, most of the time. Sometimes compasses can be inaccurate! Pilots should always bring maps when they fly, just in case.

Turn-and-Bank Indicator

Shows the plane's bank, or position, in relation to the ground. If the red ball is between the lines, the pilot is flying correctly.

Altimeter

Shows how high the plane is above sea level. The big hand tells how many hundreds of feet the plane is above sea level. The little hand shows how many thousands of feet.

Vertical Speed Indicator

Tells how fast the plane is falling or climbing. If the hand is at one, the plane is climbing 1,000 feet per minute. If the hand is at zero, the plane is level, neither climbing or falling.

Artificial Horizon

Shows where the plane is compared to the horizon. This instrument helps the pilot navigate even when the plane is flying through a cloud or heavy rain.

artificial horizon

altimeter

vertical speed indicator

HOW TO BUILD A PLANE IN 5 STEPS

1

IMAGINE

Does the idea of gliding through the clouds make you feel excited... or queasy? If you're planning on piloting, it's best not to have a fear of heights. Be brave. You might just be the next Eli Knievel. Are you up for the challenge?

2

BUILD A MODEL

It's not easy getting something heavy off the ground. Start small: Build a model. Do a test run. Does it fly? If yes, it's time to move on to bigger and better wings!

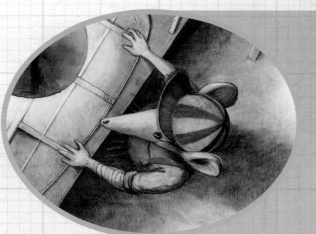

BUILD THE WINGS

As Phoebe will tell you, wings are pretty much essential when it comes to flying. Wings create lift, the force that holds an airplane in the air. Important for flying? Very!

3

BUILD THE ENGINE

The engine of a plane can be a pilot's best friend—or his worst enemy. Engine problems can lead to plane crashes! Don't let that happen to you. When you're building an engine, it's important to take your time. Triple-check your work.

4

TAKE TO THE SKY!

You did it! Welcome to life in the clouds. Don't forget to check the weather and test your navigation tools *before* you head down the runway.

5

ELI'S NEXT DREAM...